OF POLITICS AND PANDEMICS

Songs of a Russian Immigrant

· · · · · · · · · · ·

Maxim D. Shrayer

M-GRAPHICS PUBLISHING

BOSTON · 2020

Maxim D. Shrayer

Of Politics and Pandemics: Songs of Russian Immigrant

ISBN 978-1950319268

Library of Congress Control Number: 2020945063

Cover Design by Natali Cohen
Cover Photo by Maxim D. Shrayer

PUBLISHED BY M·GRAPHICS | BOSTON, MA

✉ mgraphics.books@gmail.com
🖳 www.mgraphics-publishing.com

Printed in the United States of America

The author would like to thank Boston College for its support.

*Anna Brodsky-Krotkina, Stefano Garzonio, Graeme Harper,
Karen E. Lasser, Michael Minayev, Maxim Mussel, Vera Polishchuk,
Andrew Sofer, David Shrayer-Petrov, Ekaterina Tsarapkina and Igor
Vishnevetsky read the manuscript and provided invaluable feedback.
Dobrochna Fire copyedited the manuscript with care and patience.*

The author is most grateful to them.

Contents

Depuz a mascara, e tornei a pô-la.   I took off the mask and put it back on.
Assim é melhor.   This way is better.
Assim sou a mascara.   This way I'm the mask.

Fernando Pessoa, from Poems of *Álvaro de Campos*

Лучше недо-, чем пере-.   Better to under-, then to over-.

Ilya Selvinsky, from *Anecdotes about the Karaite*
Philosopher Babakay-Sudduk

Sing low, sing high, sing wide.
Make your wit a guard and cover.
Let your laughter come free
like a help and a brace of comfort.

Carl Sandburg, "The Long Shadow
of Lincoln: A Litany"

PROLOGUE: A RUSSIAN IMMIGRANT MEETS HIS DOUBLE

1

We used to live on Beacon Street in Brookline,
the year of the election was under way,
and all the different contenders looked like

caricatures of virtue and dismay,
and yet I chose the ones I could contend with
as long as they succeeded, come what may,

in beating the Trump and rescuing our tender
democracy from a looming right-wing threat.
I knew our freedom needed a defender,

I didn't know how this theat-
rical election could be so dull,
and when I felt fed up with all the rest

I usually took our silver miniature poodle
for walks in a secluded old park,
we'd stroll around the circle and I would doodle—

with words and rhymes, and later I would park
them on my desktop, as though silly verses
could offer solace and also hit the mark

of truthfulness and justice universal—
or simply paint a picture of spring eternal.

The vernal season wasn't far ahead,
the body shunned the chill and craved the sunny
languorous days, the honey of New England.

On my long walks I would observe a skinny
bespectacled fellow with a Newfoundland
old and piebald. When the weather wasn't rainy

they occupied a bench near the sandbox where the children built their castles,
the owner read, the dog lay on the ground.

For weeks I walked my poodle round the circle
without ever speaking to the man
who seemed withdrawn or even antisocial,

who owned a dog too weak to join the clan
of other dogs careening or escaping
from their owners who knew not where they ran.

And yet I wondered: What if this is fated?
What if he's also "A Russian Immigrant,"
my own double — conjured up, created

to help me shape these lines into a rant
against tyranny, indifference, injustice,
against cruelty, contempt, intolerance?

Thus I envisaged: when he came from Russia
he brought with him a puppy: now fourteen,
he's outlived his age and broken records,

an immigrant dog the world has never seen.
I thought: the owner lived in Moscow or Saratov,
then immigrated at the age of thirty-seven

and settled in one of Boston's near suburbs,
where streets and parks resound with Russian verbs.

3

Meanwhile the Ides of March augured disaster...
The crown prince of death had crossed the Styx
and from the underworld returned to spread death faster

than doctors could invent a medical fix.
The Trump was useless. Congress dragged its feet.
And I forgot about politics.

The living life retreated. The quarantine
ruled over Boston. Zoom became our window
into the world. Imagine my esteem

for frozen spinach and for canned tomato.
We home-schooled the kids. My wife saved lives,
I taught remotely. At night I tried to veto

the hours of Netflix. Then I realized
that in pandemics arguments like mine
rang hollow, appeared oversized

especially to a keening teenage mind.
I tinkered with some writing. Nothing lofty:
I watched old Soviet movies to unwind,

I read my favorite poets: Zabolotsky,
Akhmatova, Selvinsky, Pasternak...
I went outside when the New England sky

bled colors of sunset. I headed for the park
where the dog owners maintained their social distance,
whereas the dogs refused to stay apart.

My immigrant double kept his old place
beside the sandbox now cordoned off,
he sat, a pad in hand, the Newfoundland

was dozing at his feet — sure enough
his memory was filled with greener pastures.
The immigrant dog was tired. Tired of life?

I wondered as my restless silver poodle
was pulling at her leash and urging me
to make my move, to seek out my double.

A gust of wind went through a willow tree.
I straightened my mask and slowly approached
(Please note the haunting symmetry:

Two immigrants, two dogs.) I finally broached
the subject. Indirectly. With a nod:
"Excuse me, and I don't mean to encroach

upon your privacy. Don't you find it odd
that we've been bumping into one another
without ever sharing a word

of conversation... I was wondering where in Russia
you come from?" My good double looked askance
at me, then turned his gaze in the direction

of sunset and replied, his Slavic accent
not very strong yet tangible: "My old home
has been renamed — or un-renamed, to be exact."

"St. Petersburg," I guessed. "St. Isaac's dome?"
"Yes," he confirmed. "And countless other beauties."
"I love your dog," I interjected. "He's so calm."

"He's dying," said my Russian Immigrant double.
"I'm so sorry." "No need. Now death's at everyone's door."
"I guess you're right." "I heard you dabble

in poesy." I chose to ignore
his tone. I was interested in the substance
of what he meant. "Yes, more or less. Now more

in English than in Russian." "Ha! Another instance
of trying to outdo Nabokov at his game?"
my double asked. "No, a survival instinct—

my audience is here," I came back.
"Your audience?" my double turned my statement
into a question. I was losing track

of our coded exchange. "A stalemate?"
I said, preparing to leave the park.
"Wait, please disregard my sarcasm,"

the Russian Immigrant said. "My mood is dark,
my mother's eighty-five, my dog is dying,
I'm lonely, I sit in this old park

and think about the virus." "Yes, times are trying,
we all do what we can," I said." "No, wait,"
my double asked, his own voice defying

the rules of distancing. "Can you create
a living record?" "I'm not sure what you mean."
"Can you describe this?" "This? You mean the taste

of spring on our lips? The April wind?"
"No, the pandemic," my double spoke with passion.
"The way we, immigrants, endure every kind

of destiny's tricks. But this, this is too sudden."
He turned his gaze downward, where in the sand
the local children used to play. "This is too sodden

with death. Forgive the unintended pun."
"I think I can. Been writing in a trance."
"Don't stop!" intoned my Russian Immigrant.

A mask slipped down and revealed his countenance:
a feverish smile dancing on his lips.

AN ELECTION LAMENT

The ancient senator from Vermont
is so desperate to win
he opened a second front
and joined Hezbollah and its kin.

The senior senator from Mass.
is also very keen to get
the nomination, her morass:
taxing the rich to please the rest.

The valiant mayor of South Bend, In-
diana's north, where hunters roam,
is living like a Bedouin,
campaigning all the way to Rome.

That old Pennsylvania horse,
Ukraine's friend, Ukraine's foe,
his fist is strong, his voice is hoarse,
he flies a secret UFO.

And only Amy Klobuchar
is ready to Balkanize the world,
her bluntness and Midwestern charm
are paid for with the farmers' woes.

So how do we defeat the Trump?
How we his machinations stop?
O Michael Bloomberg, lift your rump
and drink democracy's last drop.

THE DEPARTING YEAR

During the Trump impeachment
it's been difficult to smile...
This year laughing as free speech meant
more than a political style.
So we resort to Jewish jesting
bittersweet: across the sea
news of cholera in Odessa
spreads to Washington, DC.

But we don't forget the jokes
of our Soviet childhood:
When political climate chokes
it is better not to brood.
When we listen to the comments
of the clown with yellow hair
we remember happy moments,
we don't wallow in despair.

As we chime in the year
of the clever Metal Rat
we refuse to live in fear,
doctor's order: laughter, stat!

LEV AND IGOR

Lev and Igor, princely lions
gave some money to the Trump,
"I love Jews," he told them (lying),
they teared up and joined his camp.

Then they turned to dashing Rudy
who dispatched them to Ukraine,
where a scandal was gently brooding
over the end of the gravy train.

Then the Trump pressured Zelensky
and Congress said: "Investigate!"
Lev and Igor were quickly linked to
the emerging Ukrainegate.

Poor pigeons, Lev and Igor...
You've been thrown under the bus!
You're in jail now, both eager
to impeach your former boss.

Lev and Igor, cruel fortune,
A Russian Immigrant mourns your fate.
Politics is not your forte—
better stick to real estate.

Dacha Renovation

A local builder drove me around
the seaside streets of South Chatham,
ahead of us a fox traversed the road,
red tail flashing like a comet.
"That house I built three years ago
for Dr. B., a Boston surgeon.
His nephew shot himself in the garage,
they haven't visited the place since then."

We turned to Forest Beach. A seagull circled
above the turret with a copper weather cock.
"They're getting divorced. A custody battle.
What can I say... my customers have bad luck."
We slowly drove uphill. It started to rain.
"You see that house with a widow's walk?
I built it for a family from Maine... "
"Please stop the truck," I said, "I'm walking back."

PETER BEINART'S DEPARTURE

There was a time (we thought it was behind us)
when Communists sincerely maintained
that Stalin's crimes were, well... not so heinous
and then apologized for Soviet mistakes.

Thus *Jewish Currents* flowed into oblivion
until it rediscovered its old part...
Its flag was then repainted vermillion,
its music was still Soviet at heart.

Directives no longer came from Moscow
yet they inherited the Soviet rhetoric
of anti-Zionism; and then their news bureau
decided to recruit a Menshevik.

O Peter Beinart, your trajectory is sobering,
your "crisis of Zionism" has rendered you obtuse.
What's next in your career as a Soviet—
a column in *Pravda* or a stint in *Gaza News*?

The Senate Trial

I often think about the Trump,
victory blaring from his trunk,
the Constitution's butcher...

His loyal senators behave
like lazy generals who hate
to ponder their future.

He'll probably get away this time.
Imposing, elephantine,
he stomps out his critics...

In our history's own court
will he remain the tweeting sort,
the brazen face of politics?

DREAMING OF MR. YANG

I had a dream that Mr. Yang
has joined Chabad and grown *peyes*,
he davens with his whole gang
and only dines at kosher places.
He now argues that the Chinese
descended from the Tribe of Simeon—
across the desert and seven seas
they traveled all the way to Xi'an.

He changed his name to "Yankelman,"
an ardent Zionist, Israel's defender,
and Bernie's ratings all went down,—
who needs a socialist self-hater?
I woke up and checked the news,
Bari Weiss gives Yang a big thumps up,
he'll get the votes of many Jews
as long as he defeats the Trump.

THE DEBATES, OR SIX HOOLIGANS

Six candidates decided to debate
who's best prepared to defeat the T.
Their rules were simple: we shall not debase
each other's presidential quality.

At once the junior senator from Vermont
deployed his vitriol: "Former Mayor, go chase
your billions, Wallstreet's your storefront,
the Cayman Islands are your home base."

Then went the senior senator from Massachusetts, adding insult to burning fire:
"You racist scum, you sexist pig, your ads
won't buy you this election, go expire."

The mayor of South Bend attacked
the Minnesotan retrograde:
"You don't know Mexico from scat,
you failed geography, go back to second grade."

The Slovene senator didn't hold back:
"You calling me dumb? You think this shit will stick?
I'll show you who's more gay and black,
you mamma's boy, you little prick."

The old Vice President became irate,
so he decided to unload his chagrin:
"I love the Jews, but two in one debate?
I love gay people, but we're here to win."

The former mayor of New York stood straight
and tried to look unscathed although he
was getting angry at his fellow Democrats
for fighting dirty and escaping scot-free.

He finally spoke: "This is America, my friends,
I made my billions with my own hands.
So what's your problem, you don't have a pair of pants,
and now the others should go without pants?"

He then continued: "I had a nickname coined
for each of you: 'self-hating Jew,' 'fake Indian,'
'old Philly steak,' 'corn belt diva,' 'drama queen,'
I will employ them in my ad campaign."

Then things got really messy: throwing eggs,
fist-fighting, swearing—and forgetting
that he just gloated, an invincible T-Rex,
and rubbed his pinkish hands.

HERE'S TO BIDEN'S VICTORY AT SOUTH CAROLINA

Joe finally took South Carolina:
Hurray, *vivat*, and *bozhe moy*!
A Democratic ocean liner
delivered Obama's last envoy
to Charlestown Harbor, where a crowd
was chanting "Our best days
still lie ahead..." I stood and frowned:
Best days? Ahead? A hollow phrase.

Can Joe defeat the Trump, I wondered
while sipping a very sweet iced tea.
And then I thought: Our days are numbered,
the whole election a travesty.
The Democrats, my old fortress—
divided, tired, superweak—
I'll vote, of course, but who to vote for?
My Super Tuesday's looking bleak.

A Farewell to Pete Buttigieg

Farewell, my Pete, the country isn't ready
to follow your clear, articulate style…
Your rise was meteoric, outrageous,
how young you are to go into exile.

You were a falcon among the common avians,
you flew direct from Malta to South Bend,
you charmed suburban moms and immigrant parents,
your tie was loose, your gait was elegant.

Cry, Russian Hoosiers, your hero's decided
to leave the race; he was too good for that.
He didn't beat the Trump; so now it's Biden
or Bloomberg or another old hat…

TO SENATOR SANDERS: AN OPEN LETTER

My dear Sanders, *zai a mensch* (not that you really know
Yiddish) and show the world what you meant was to defeat
the Trump and finish. Like Pete and Amy, be astute, leave
now, clear the field for Biden and Harris, or another suit of
winning candidates. Abandon your revolutionary life, and
disavow your Soviet training; there's time, o Bernie, to alight
from the campaign that you're draining. But if you stubbornly
want to fight and if your Marxist heart is aching, go take
a Transsiberian flight: there's North Korea for the taking.

On Running into a Former Neighbor
at the Charlottesville Airport

Your hallowed dream of owning a house—
nine yards of grass, a hammock and a swing—
has been achieved, so celebrate and sing,
don't lock yourself inside, don't howl.
You've realized your bourgeois ambition...
A leafy suburb offers an escape
from everything you hated growing up—
oh how you dread their poverty and pain.

Your father's business, flat, deflated, burning,
your sister's welfare check, poor diet, Virginia drawl...
You've married up: Bostonian, old school,
your children won't feel your shame and yearning.
You stare your former neighbor in the temple,
you'd shoot him, if you could, but where's your gun?
Your world is gone, shopkeeperess, your temple
of Trumpian hopes has come undone.

Ode to Absurdity

Coronavirus crowns your lifespan,
Corovavirus serves your latte,
Corozovirus carves your buttons,
Corojovirus rolls your smokes.

The Trump pretends he didn't know
that viruses could be so lethal
and millions (that included grandpa)
had perished from the Spanish flu.

Meantime the candidates infect us
with sluggishness and hopeless banter,
their videos just won't go viral,
their slogans only irritate.

Our country, like a drunken cruise ship,
is sailing toward the great pandemic,
I'm running out of disinfectant,
and only vodka clears the soul.

Look Homeward and Recoil

for Anna Brodsky-Krotkina

I heard Ms. Tereshkova at the Duma,
her face was shiny and her perm was iron-clad,
the speech she gave couldn't be any dumber,
I listened and I thought: boy, am I glad
that we gave up this paradise of Soviet ladies
who wear party suits and hate the West,
who breathlessly live into their eighties
like mad *matreshka*s fallen out of the nest.

She was the first, the glorious *kosmonavtka*,
but not the first to dress the Leader's arse
with kisses though she wasn't a nut case,
her speech was not a constitutional farce.
Her message was: the foreign agents send us
their viruses across the airspace,
we need a mighty ruler to defend us,
Tsar Vladimir will shield us from disgrace.

I watched the speech by Valentina Tereshkova,
she looked so good, her eyes so brutally kind,
she was a perfectly post-Soviet cover
for everything we immigrants left behind.

TWEETS AND SHOUTS

1

A Russian Immigrant who stands
at a New England graveyard feels the danger
of loneliness because he is a stranger
uncovered by these snows, unrooted in these sands.

2

O Monday morning, morning of damnation,
The Trump's administration eats our nation,
the Senate drinks its mug of indecision;
and we the people, do we have a vision?

3

The passing of the day,
the mummery and tricks,
the sunset spilt like hay
on century-old tracks...

4

You did your taxes and you paid your dues.
Now what? The system wins, you lose.
It's almost April, a chilly afternoon;
your fiscal afterlife is coming soon.

Go Clamming and Recite Russian Poetry

for M. and T.

At low tide I bring my daughters
where the ocean meets the pond,
we call this area "Three Waters,"
beyond it lies Nantucket Sound.

We join a troop of local pickers
digging the yellow sandbar;
in our parti-colored slickers
we look like tourists though we are

Bostonians. The virus, dreadful,
has sent us running to the Cape,
in Chatham we've taken refuge,
this dacha is our last escape.

How long we'll last? G-d only knows,
the clams lie buried in the mud,
the sun is bright, the panic grows,
G-d grant that we don't go mad...

How to Practice Social Distancing

I'm distanced socially from
both Rabbi Marx and Rabbi Freud.

I left my regular workplace
and labor at my own pace.

Now I lecture via Zoom
about Chekhov's dusk and gloom.

I wear old jeans and keds,
I homeschool my own kids.

I kiss my wife across six feet,
my world is shrinking tweet by tweet.

I hug my friends via Facebook,
it feels absurd but what the fuck.

COVID-19 is my confrère,
I'm ready, I'm prepared, I'm there...

Forget Weltschmerz in the Midst of a Pandemic

How could it be that I no longer care
that Biden won the Democratic race,
and Sanders lost—thus ending his career
as socialist pain in the rear,
and sparing us utopian disgrace?

How could it be that now I only care
about you, my family and friends?
It happened overnight, I simply stare
the future in the face and see a fleer
acknowledging my own indifference.

The past two weeks have dispossessed my psyche
of false pretentions and gentility,
I've lost the key to pain and melancholy...
Have I returned to being a refugee?

WARDING OFF DESPAIR

for mama and papa

I can't convince my parents to stay
indoors and follow the quarantine.
They say: "Don't isolate us." "Ah, touché!"

I can't convince my daughter who's fourteen
that patience is a virtue, and the world
will soon recover and become pristine.

I can't convince my daughter who is twelve
that Levin's love for Kitty is not a lie,
and Vronsky's love for Anna is not a poisoned well.

I can't convince myself the plague is nigh,
and we should hastily evacuate
to the deep country where we could survive.

I can't convince my wife it's not too late
to load our things into a makeshift ark
and sail off toward an unknown fate.

And so what's left? The pharmacy, the bank,
the Russian store, take out: Japanese,
the park, the soccer field, the riverbank,

the puffy clouds, the sun, the ocean breeze...
I'm still alive. Not down on my knees.

Lenin liked the Moonlight Sonata and Swiss penknives,
Stalin liked plays by Bulgakov and funerals of old Bolsheviks,
Khrushchev liked corn on the cob and abstract painting,
Brezhnev liked young nurses and boar hunting,
Andropov liked chamber theater and lawn tennis,
Chernenko liked black holes and Siberian dumplings,
Gorbachev liked failed empires and Louis Vuitton bags,
Yeltsin liked any kind of vodka and brass bands,
Putin liked pestilence and silence.

A PRAYER FOR ITALY

for Stefano Garzonio

Death dares not rhyme with Italy,
for Italy only rhymes with *vita*—
perhaps not always sweet, yet vibrantly
alive, beloved, undefeated.

To Russian Jews this love came free,
here we spent our Roman holiday,
we rested, one foot in Ladispoli,
the other in America's doorway.

O Italy, who will steal your bicycles
and rent Umberto D.'s old lodgings?
Milan, devoid of your miracles
the world feels so lonely.

What use are verses of remembrance
when the Italian earth is trembling,
when Bergamo, like a frenzied ambulance,
is racing to its day of reckoning?

The Tiber meets the sea at Ostia,
the Arno sleeps at Ponte Vecchio.
These broken rhymes, a feeble offering...
My friends in Italy, I pray for you.

Evacuation (An Homage to Daniil Kharms)

If in my Soviet childhood
I'd heard this episode,
I'd think that in all likelihood
I'd think that in all likelihood
'twas utterly absurd.

A Russian Immigrant put his kids
and wife into the car,
his plan was to escape COVID
his plan was to escape COVID
by moving not too far.

They quickly realized: their hound
by accident stayed behind,
they turned around
they turned around
and went back to Brookline.

They drove across the empty fields
on a desolate highway,
a runaway feels
a runaway feels
the way they felt that day.

"Don't worry, guys," the Immigrant said,
cheering up his family.
"The Cape is safe
the Cape is safe,
at the dacha we'll be free."

State Trooper stopped them at the bridge
and asked them who they were,
they felt on edge
they felt on edge
but tried not to demur.

Then at the supermarket where
they'd shopped for many years,
the cashier's stare
the cashier's stare
confirmed their worst fears.

Around the corner from their lane
a town cop pulled them over,
"What brings you down?
What brings you down?"
he asked them with a glower.

"Our place is here," they replied,
"our taxes fund your school."
They really tried to be polite
they really tried to be polite,
tried hard to keep their cool.

That evening as they walked their hound
a neighbor accosted them,
"You bring your Boston germs around
you bring your Boston germs around
and spread 'em in our town."

Our Immigrant wanted to transplant
his family to Cape Cod,
but now he worries that his plan
but now he worries that his plan
will do them little good.

He sleeps all day, he guards all night
his family and homestead,
his rifle is loaded all right
his rifle is loaded but his heart,
his heart is filled with dread.

La Chanson des Chiens

Dogs in the park maintain the proper distance,
they probably sense the owners' reluctance

to come together and take an open stance
against the power of happenstance.

The park is like a hospital; with masks on
the people's faces hide their contagion,

yet every walker in the park could be an agent
of the mysterious, virulent invasion.

Some canine partners look quite attractive
in their masks and gloves, hence the protective

attire has become the new elective
affinity, a fashion for the restive.

The weeping willows clench their greening lancets,
to them, of course, the human drama is senseless,

with our dogs, in our silly dresses
we look incredibly defenseless.

Life in the park is growing distant, static;
we stand apart and talk: an Irish medic,

a Russian Immigrant, a Parisian academic.
Another day of the pandemic...

A RESPONSE TO A PETITION BY CAPE COD RESIDENTS

Concerned Citizens of Cape Cod:
Why do you want to close the bridges
and isolate yourselves from the world?
Why do you act like a secret police squad
instead of welcoming strangers?

Angry Citizens of Cape Cod:
Why do you blame New Yorkers for the shortage of flour,
washashores for the dearth of trout in kettle ponds,
Bostonians for traffic on Route 28,
and people with foreign accents for your own fear?

Terrified Citizens of Cape Cod,
please hear it from a refugee:
Illness only knows flesh and blood.
Illness spares no race or creed,
no income or identity.

Fair Citizens of Cape Cod:
Do you blame the sky for heavy rain,
the moon for high tide,
the sun for cold days?
Do you blame G-d?

FAMILY HAPPINESS IN FIVE PARTS

for K.

You played the cello at a classmate's wedding...
It was a hot September in Vermont
many years ago. The girls had not been born
though we were trying. Desperately? Not
so much, not yet — the happy ending
obliterates the memory of want.

You played the cello in a sage green outfit,
sleeves flowing on the mountain air.
I don't remember what you played. Glière?
Or was it Bruch? Some long-forgotten tier
of melodies, a hideaway, an orbit
where hours were long, arms bare.

You played the cello, but it was your old cello,
the one the cleaners dropped and cracked.
An accident. It had to be replaced.
We bought a German make, it played
so lustrously that we abandoned the yellow
old maple body though we kept the strings...

The married classmate is no longer a kindred spirit,
though once a month you see her at grand rounds.
Our daughters now make their own daily rounds,
replete with teenage sites and sounds,
and only rarely do you and I revisit
the places where the past rebounds.

In those memories you play and smile faintly,
your fingers stir like pebbles in the brook,
your bow unlocks the long-forgotten songbook
in which we lived, anticipating the daily
Tolstoyan miracle, the promise of a family,
Five years. Sixty months. All it took.

BOSTON BLUES

Do people really need all their poets,
No more than they need their cripples...
David Shrayer-Petrov

Some fucking nut
stands outside the local CVS
and tells each customer: "Now the middle class
has tasted what it's like."

Another fucking nut
stands in the briefing room
and tells each citizen: "You must
take hydroxychloroquine."

A senator from Vermont
stands somewhere on Lake Champlain
and tells his fellow nuts:
"I won't quit the campaign."

An old chestnut tree
stands at my street corner,
its crown is barely green,
it's dying of corona.

My inner fucking nut
stands at his mental podium
composing with his gut
what sounds like a poem.

PHILANTHROPIC AND A BIT MISANTHROPIC

All are sick, and the pharmacy's triumphant...
Nikolay Nekrasov

A local symphony orchestra is calling
to ask for my support:
I order a CD of Mozart's Requiem,
Andris Nelsons conducting.

A local Russian bookstore is calling
to solicit my support:
I donate money to help with rent,
my eyes rolling.

A local dry cleaner is calling
to enlist my support:
I buy a mask from them, hand-made,
to wear while strolling.

A local Thai place is calling
to encourage my support:
I order a take-out,
Som Tam and Tom Yum Goong.

A local gym is calling
to beg for my support:
I work out to my heart's content
while staring at their Zoom link.

And only the pharmacy is calling
to tell me all my meds are in.
I scream into the phone receiver:
"You, pharmacist, don't triumph."
And I refuse to rhyme and meter with the Trump.

SENTIMENTAL EDUCATION

for Katya and Maxim

Soviet women past their prime
in aubergine turtlenecks washed to sheen,
Vera Josephovna Pearlbaum,
Lubov Leonidovna Burnstein.

Public detractors of Stalin,
secret admirers of Pasternak,
keepers of old family cooking style,
cloves and garlic, celery and parsnips.

"Dear children, you must love the classics,"
they preached in voices laced with pain
as our masters shot down a South Korean liner
west of Sakhalin in the Sea of Japan.

"The English teacher, she's no dummy," spoke one classmate.
"Jews are usually smart." I stared out the window.
"Fucking Russian teacher," spoke another classmate.
"The sniveling Jewbitch." I smashed the window.

"All the world's a stage, and we're merely players,"
repeated Vera Williamovna Pearstein.
"Children, drop by drop, squeeze out the slave,"
repeated Lubov Antonovna Burnbaum.

Outside the window the warmhearted playboy Brezhnev was dying,
after him the bloodthirsty spymaster Andropov was dying,
after him the timid party secretary Chernenko was dying,
then Gorbachev fought for his spot under the sun of the dying.

We read "Lady with Lapdog" we memorized Shakespeare's sonnets,
we learned to love and betray one another.
A whole lifetime wouldn't be enough
to shake the memories of this rancorous theater.

Rethinking Labor Relations

Well, Karl Marx is probably turning
or laughing in his English grave,
while Leo Tolstoy is returning
to his old saw: work shall save.
The cleaners don't clean at this hour
of lockdown, and the handymen refuse
to repair our toilet and shower,
to replace a malfunctioning fuse.

I'm constantly cleaning and fixing,
and I have no time to create
a new murderist manifesto
or a classic of brotherly hate.
Now if there's courage to muster,
and if there's a lesson to learn:
When man can no longer save master
how can master save man?

A NEAR-LIMERICK

(authoritative version)

There was once an old leech
who OD'd on some bleach,
    but he wanted his electorate to suffer,
    he pretentiously wept, then maniacally went
back to tweeting the word IMPEACH.

(alternative version)

There was once an old leech
who OD'd on some bleach
    and, deciding to make his friends suffer,
    he hysterically wept, then courageously went
for more bleach to the nearest drugstore.

THAT SCAPEGOATING MAYOR

When a mayor scapegoats
a group of his town's Jews
gathered at a rabbi's funeral
in the midst of a pandemic,
the long history of Judeophobia
comes blazingly alive
and haunts both the town
and the whole country.

PSYCHOANALYSIS DURING A PANDEMIC

He gives a sign, and all go fussing
                                        Pushkin

Speak not, lie hidden and conceal
                        Tyutchev, tr. Nabokov

A fox came by this afternoon
impersonating Jacques Lacan—
or was it Jung, I wasn't sure,
the fox looked Swiss and very mature.

He summoned me to lie prostrate
in my back yard and liberate
my bound speech to let it flow,
revealing everything I know.

On my back I lay like a corpse,
the fox invaded my soul by force,
it scoped me with its long red nose
while its tail formed a noose

around my neck. The fox insisted:
"Submit yourself, don't stay clenched-fisted."
He tortured me and took me captive
to where unconscious was collective.

"Stop, Dr. Fox, I'm not your patient,
I won't be part of your equation,
I need my soul in times of crisis
when isolation drives one crazy."

The fox slipped out of his frock coat
becoming an embodiment of
my COVID angst, my sleepless dreams
in which the iambs lose their schemes.

CHOLERA IN CRIMEA

And I remember a photo: a military
Man, clean-shaven like a billiards ball
Genrikh Sapgir

I don't remember the epidemic, just the panic:
August 1970, Sebastopol, the smell
of rotting apricots, my mother's dainty tunic,
Uchkuevka beach, the cotton heat, the groundswell

of fear. Seething lines at the ticket office,
vacationers like wartime evacuees.
The talk of spreading illness. Words like "orifice"
or "dehydration" hanging in the breeze.

The hasty packing. My collection of stag beetles
forgotten on the windowsill. Our train
arriving at Kursk Station. Empty bottles.
My parents kissing on the platform. Reunion.

I didn't know another parting was near:
my father, a doctor, would be dispatched to Crimea.

Taking Stock of the Past Five Months

There is nothing more to say
Edwin Arlington Robinson

The world makes no sense:
Over the past five months
it's lost its innocence.

We've learned the art of distance,
we've mastered wearing masks;
the world makes no sense,

we're living in a trance,
without its daily tasks
it's lost its innocence.

What happened to the scents
of life and simple tastes?
The world makes no sense,

what do we tell ourselves:
that our world is nuts,
it's lost its innocence?

Will we regain our strength?
Will we recover our wits?
The world makes no sense,
it's lost its innocence.

Epilogue: A Russian Immigrant Tires
of the Quarantine in Boston

They started the day as husband and wife
and parted at night as brother and sister,
Boston had tired of constant worry,
spring was scorched to the ground by the virus,
and the April city-wide disaster
was becoming May-bound melancholy.

They stared at life outside the window
when heavy rain came down from the sky;
they circled their block on Beacon Street
when the blazing sunset hung low and wide;
the strolling white masks terrified,
the running black masks stopped their hearts.

The T flitted off, long and taciturn,
the empty cars looked countless,
we stopped and ogled, like refugees,—
dogs and birds, elms and chestnut trees,
old women and children, newspaper rats—
life had nowhere else to turn.

December 2019—June 2020
Brookline and South Chatham, Massachusetts

Notes on the Text

"…Akhmatova, Selvinsky, Pasternak…"—a reader of Russian modernist poetry will recognize a distinct echo of "Tikhonov, Selvinsky, Pasternak" from Eduard Bagritsky's 1927 "A Conversation with the Komsomol Member N. Dementiev" (Razgovor s komsomol'tsem N. Dement'evym). See also an allusion to Anna Akhmatova's *Requiem* later in the text of the Prologue.

Lev Parnas and Igor Fruman—American businessmen of Jewish Soviet origin. The Russian first name "Lev" (from the Germanic "Löwe") means "lion." Prince Igor I ruled Kievan Rus sometime between 912 and 945, the exact span of his rule still subject to scholarly debate. **Rudy**—Rudy Giuliani, former mayor of New York.

Volodymyr Zelensky—President of Ukraine, elected in 2019.

Peter Alexander Beinart—American journalist and political polemicist, author of *The Crisis of Zionism* (2012) and columnist for the magazine *Jewish Currents*.

Andrew M. Yang—American entrepreneur, lawyer, and philanthropist. A Democratic presidential candidate, Yang dropped out of the race on 11 February 2020.

Bari Weiss—American journalist, a former staff editor of *The New York Times* opinion page; author of *How to Fight Anti-Semitism* (2019).

Hurray, *vivat* and ***bozhe moy***!—*bozhe moy* = my G-d (Russian).

Corovavirus — from the Russian *korova* = cow; corozovirus — from the corozo (tagua nut), from which buttons and jewelry are made; **corojovirus** — from corojo, a type of tobacco.

Zai a mensch — Yiddish for "be a [good] man [person]."

Valentina Tereshkova — Soviet cosmonaut, in 1963 the first and youngest woman to fly solo in space; presently a member of the Russian national Duma from the United Russia party. *Matreshka* — Russian nestling doll. *Kosmonavtka* — Russian (with a bit of an edge) for female cosmonaut.

"G-d grant that we don't go mad..." (Ne dai mne Bog soiti s uma)—the opening line of Aleksandr Pushkin's untitled poem of 1833.

Levin... Kitty... Vronsky... Anna — characters in Tolstoy's *Anna Karenina*.

"For Italy only rhymes with vita" — the poem contains references to Italian films of the 1940s-1960s, directed by Luchino Visconti, Vittorio De Sica, and Federico Fellini, and a reference to an American film directed by William Wyler and set in Rome. **Ladispoli** — town on the Tyrrhenian Coast, 35 kilometers west of Rome. In the 1970s and 1980s, tens of thousands of former Soviet Jews and their families stayed in Ladispoli while waiting for their visas to enter the United States and other destinations. This experience is depicted in Maxim D. Shrayer's literary memoir *Waiting for America: A Story of Emigration*.

Daniil Kharms — an early Soviet Russian-language poet and children's author in the absurdist vein; arrested in August 1941 for disseminating a "libelous and defeatist spirit," Kharms died of inanition in a prison psychiatric ward during the siege of

Leningrad. One of Kharms's most famous poems is "A men once left his own home..." (Iz doma vyshel chelovek...).

...a Petition by Cape Cod Residents — in March 2020 residents of Cape Cod circulated a petition to close the bridges so as to prevent incoming traffic to Cape Cod and thereby restrict the influx of COVID-19.

"Do people really need all their poets,/ No more than they need their cripples..." (Nuzhny li poety narodu? /Ne bolee, chem urody... — from the poem "Poets and Cripples" (Poety i urody) by David Shrayer-Petrov.

"All are sick, and the pharmacy's triumphant..." (Vse bol'ny, torzhestvuet apteka...)—the fifth line in part two of Nikolay Nekrasov long poem *About Weather* (*O pogode*, 1858–59).

Vera Josephovna... Lubov Leonidovna... Vera Williamovna... Lubov Antonovna — the patronymics come from the first names Joseph (as in Joseph Stalin), Leonid (as in Leonid Pasternak, the father of Boris Pasternak), William (as in William Shakespeare) and Anton (as in Anton Chekhov). **"Our masters shot down a South Korean liner..."**—on 1 September 1983 a Soviet interceptor plane shot down and destroyed Korean Air Lines Flight 007 en route from Anchorage to Seoul, killing all the passengers on board.

"When a mayor scapegoats..."—the reference is to the comments New York City mayor Bill de Blasio made on 28 April 2020 about a Hasidic Jewish funeral in Brooklyn. De Blasio later apologized, sort of.

"He gives a sign, and all go fussing" (On znak podast — i vse khlopochut)—the opening line of stanza 18 of chapter 5 of Aleksandr Puhskin's novel in verse *Eugene Onegin* (1823–30; book 1833).

In Tatiana's vatic, phantasmagoric dream, "he" refers to Onegin, and the death of Lensky by Onegin's hand at a duel is prefigured.

"Speak not, lie hidden and conceal/the way you dream, the things you feel…" (Molchi, skryvaisa i tai/ I chuvstva i mechty svoi…)—the opening lines of Fyodor Tyutchev's programmatic poem "Silentium" (1829, early 1830s), translated by Vladimir Nabokov for *Three Russian Poets* (1943).

"And I remember a photo: a military/ Man, clean-shaven like a billiards ball" (Ia pomniu fotografiiu: voennyi/ Do bleska vybrit — kak bil'iardnyi shar)—last two lines of the first quatrain of Genrikh Sapgir's sonnet "A Landscape with the Artists' Colony at Bolshevo" from the collection *Sonnets on Shirts* (Sonety na rubash-kakh, 1978).

Dedications and Acknowledgements

To Stella the silver poodle,
who's faithful, kind, and noble
and barks like a perfect angel.

To my courageous daughters,
who braved the cold waters
of Mill Creek in late April.

To my amazing parents,
who weathered the viral torrents
in their Brookline sanctum.

But most of all to Karen,
whose name shall not be stolen
and turned into a slang term.

I love you with all my might,

(Signed)

A Russian Immigrant

Index of Names and Places

He did it all just to impress her:
translator, author, and professor
at Boston College, where he studies
a number of areas while he saddles
three horses: Russian, English, and Jewish,
he teaches everything you wish
to know about exile and love
(read *Yom Kippur in Amsterdam*),
about immigrants in transit
(his *Waiting for America* is it),
about Jewish-Russian writers
(whose voices he has long curated).
His work has generated some hype
and gained a hefty Guggenheim.
(Please see more info on his site
or follow his tweets, however trite.)
A former Muscovite and refusenik
he's lived in Boston for twenty-five years
and in America for almost
3.5 decades, not a minor feat.
His hero, *A Russian Immigrant*,
has lately moved to the forefront
of Maxim D. Shrayer's creative tide,
like his creator, he resides
in Brookline, Mass. with wife and kids
and has a house on Cape Cod;
unlike his master, he does not
aspire to offer profound thought.
A Russian Immigrant entertains
with Jewish humor in his veins,
Russian soul-searching in his rimes,
American optimism in bad times.

Photo: Lee Pellegrini

Praise for Maxim D. Shrayer's *Of Politics and Pandemics*

"The author, or rather his Russian immigrant lyrical hero, regards poetry as a fainting mirror of doubles, in which boundaries of time and space are erased. Reality and memory, everyday life and the absolute of destiny, feelings, fears and hopes, the pandemic present and the historical past are all split apart and reconnected in the course of Shrayer's poetical dialogue with himself and others. Both apocalyptic banality and existential suspense need a special poetic perspective: '...Can you create/ a living record? I'm not sure what you mean./ Can you describe this? This? You mean the taste/ of spring on our lips? The April wind?/ No, the pandemic, my double spoke with passion.' This dialogue recalls Anna Akhmatova's tragic words in *Requiem*: 'Can you describe this? And I said: I can.'"

— **Stefano Garzonio**, Professor of Slavic Studies, Pisa University, editor of *Poesia Russa* (2004) and *Lirici Russi dell'Ottocento* (2011)

"Whether lobbing satiric barbs at presidential hopefuls or pondering the bonds of marriage and family in a time of pandemic, Maxim D. Shrayer's collection, at once lyrical and playful, captures the predicament of a Russian immigrant in Trump-era America with delicious wit and timely acuity."

— **Andrew Sofer**, poet and Professor of English, of Boston College, author of *Wave* and *Dark Matter*

"Maxim D. Shrayer's new collection of poems is a splendid achievement, and just what the doctor ordered for readers reeling from the double assault of political upheavals and raging pandemic. Shrayer's poems are not only personal, but also culturally rich and politically astute — a rare combination in lyric poetry. The poet-narrator, a melancholy, sometimes self-ironizing sophisticate, is a Russian émigré steeped in the tradition of European literature, and profoundly familiar, from first-hand experience, with what an autocratic regime looks like. His otherness is the source of funny, sane, penetrating observations about events in America in 2020. Maxim D. Shrayer's *Of Politics and Pandemics* is a tonic for our times."

> — **Anna Brodsky-Krotkina**, Professor of Russian Studies,
> Washington & Lee University
> and columnist, *Nezavisimaya gazeta*

"I like humor. As the philosopher once said, 'I find it funny.' And there is plenty to turn a smile in this collection. At points I even found myself laughing out loud. Only soon after to be confronted with moments of deep despair. You can't live in America at the moment and not find yourself taken aback by the laughable craziness of some things and the incredible desperation of others. Maxim D. Shrayer captures that feeling so well. Without much fanfare, he also makes an urgent case for the thinking person and for a return to decency and civility in our leaders—to which I say: here's to that!"

> — **Graeme Harper**, Editor, *New Writing: the International Journal for the Practice and Theory of Creative Writing*
> and author of *Discovering Creative Writing*

Printed in Great Britain
by Amazon